How to Draw the Life and Times of
John F. Kennedy

Dulce Zamora

The Rosen Publishing Group's
PowerKids Press™
New York

To Nina and Francis
No matter what, we've always got each other.

Published in 2006 by The Rosen Publishing Group, Inc.
29 East 21st Street, New York, NY 10010

First Edition

Editor: Rachel O'Connor
Layout Design: Elana Davidian
Photo Researcher: Jeffrey Wendt

Illustrations: All illustrations by Albert Hanner.
Photo Credits: p. 4 Snark/Art Resource, NY; p. 7 akg-images; p. 9 © Brooks Kraft/Corbis; p. 10
Courtesy National Park Service, John F. Kennedy National Historic Site; p. 12 PT Boats, Inc; p. 14
© David J. & Janice L. Frent Collection/Corbis; p. 16 Paul Schutzer/Time Life Pictures/Getty Images;
p. 18 Courtesy the Peace Corps; pp. 18, 24, 28 © Bettmann/Corbis; p. 20 © Corbis; p. 22 Getty
Images; p. 26 © Larry Downing/Reuters/Corbis.

Library of Congress Cataloging-in-Publication Data

Zamora, Dulce.
How to draw the life and times of John Fitzgerald Kennedy / Dulce Zamora.— 1st ed.
p. cm. — (A kid's guide to drawing the presidents of the United States of America) Includes index.
ISBN 1-4042-3011-4 (lib. bdng.)
1. Kennedy, John F. (John Fitzgerald), 1917–1963—Juvenile literature. 2. Presidents—United States—
Biography—Juvenile literature. 3. Drawing—Technique—Juvenile literature. I. Title. II. Series.
E842.Z9Z36 2006
973.922'092—dc22

2005014950

Printed in China

Contents

Young Kennedy

John Fitzgerald Kennedy, also known as JFK, led the United States from 1961 to 1963. These years were filled with problems in America and throughout the world. JFK was never afraid of facing these problems, though.

JFK was always interested in current events. As a high-school student at the Choate School in Wallingford, Connecticut, he read the *New York Times* every day. This was not something many teenagers did. Kennedy attended Choate from 1931 to 1935. In 1936, he went to Harvard University. He was in London in September 1939, when Germany attacked Poland. England and France declared war against Germany soon after. This was the beginning of World War II. Kennedy thought England made mistakes leading up to the war, and he wrote a paper about it. He turned it into a book called *Why England Slept*. The book made him famous. He joined the U.S. Navy and survived a 1943 Japanese attack on his boat in the South Pacific, which added to his fame.

Soon Kennedy entered politics as a member of the Democratic Party. He served as a Massachusetts congressman from 1947 to 1953, and as a senator from 1953 to 1960. In 1957, he won a Pulitzer Prize for his book *Profiles in Courage.*

In 1960, Kennedy decided to run for president of the United States as a Democratic candidate. He beat Vice President Richard Nixon, the Republican candidate. At 43 years old, Kennedy became the youngest man ever to be elected U.S. president. His wife, Jacqueline Bouvier Kennedy, whom he had married in 1953, became First Lady at 31 years old.

You will need the following supplies to draw the life and times of John F. Kennedy:

✓ A sketch pad   ✓ An eraser   ✓ A pencil   ✓ A ruler

These are some of the shapes and drawing terms you need to know:

Horizontal Line	——	Squiggly Line	∿
Oval	⬭	Trapezoid	⏢
Rectangle	▭	Triangle	△
Shading	▬	Vertical Line	|
Slanted Line	/	Wavy Line	～

A Short but Full Life

As president of the United States, John F. Kennedy tackled many big issues at home and overseas. One major accomplishment was avoiding a nuclear war with the Soviet Union. The Soviet Union was a group of 15 territories in eastern Europe and central Asia that was ruled by one Communist government. The Soviets and the Americans both had nuclear arms. Each feared that the other would use the weapons. In 1963, Soviet leader Nikita Khrushchev and JFK settled on an agreement to limit testing of nuclear weapons.

In the United States in the 1960s, there were protests against unfair treatment of African Americans. JFK tried to protect these protesters against angry crowds. Yet many African American leaders said he had not done enough to advance civil rights. Kennedy was able to make many of these leaders happy in 1963 by proposing a civil rights bill that secured equal treatment for all Americans. However, the bill did not pass during JFK's lifetime. Kennedy was shot and killed in Dallas, Texas, on November 22, 1963.

John F. Kennedy is shown here speaking to the people of New York during his 1960 election campaign. His wife, Jacqueline Bouvier Kennedy, is by his side.

John F. Kennedy's Massachusetts

Massachusetts

The John F. Kennedy Library and Museum opened in 1979.

Map of the United States of America

Massachusetts was an important place in John F. Kennedy's life. He was born there in 1917. The five-bedroom house where he was born is in Brookline, Massachusetts. More than one million people have visited the home since it became a historical site, or area, in 1967. Public tours are available. People can see the bed in which John, or Jack as he was also known, was born. They can also see his silver baby bowl, and other things the family owned while they lived at the house.

The Kennedy family moved to New York when Jack was about 10 years old, but they continued to spend summers in Massachusetts. In 1929, Kennedy's father, Joseph, bought a house with a lawn and private beach in Hyannis Port, Massachusetts. Jack and his brothers and sisters loved to swim, sail, and play football there. When JFK grew up, he continued to spend time in Hyannis Port with his wife and children.

In Boston a statue of Kennedy stands outside the west wing of the Massachusetts State House. The statue, created by artist Isabel McIlvain, was officially dedicated on what would have been Kennedy's seventy-third birthday, May 29, 1990. More details about President Kennedy's life can be found at the John F. Kennedy Library and Museum in Boston. It opened on October 20, 1979.

This statue of JFK, created by Isabel McIlvain, stands outside the Massachusetts State House. The artist chose to show Kennedy walking.

Young Jack

On May 29, 1917, John Kennedy was born in an upstairs bedroom of his family's wooden home in Brookline, a town just west of Boston. Jack was the second of nine children born to Joseph and Rose Kennedy. As a child Jack had scarlet fever, chicken pox, asthma,

and other illnesses. His health did not improve as he got older, but he never let sickness stop him from playing football or joining the swim team.

Jack's family was wealthy. Their wealth allowed Jack to attend some of America's best private schools. These included the Choate School, in Wallingford, Connecticut, the high school he entered in 1931. In 1936, he entered Harvard University in Cambridge, Massachusetts. Although Kennedy went to fine schools, he was at first more interested in sports and friends than in his studies. He studied harder after traveling to Europe a few times between 1937 and 1939. Political issues there interested him, and he wanted to learn as much as he could about world affairs.

1

You are going to draw the house where John Kennedy was born. Begin the drawing of the house with a rectangle. This will be your guide.

2

Draw the roof at the top of the rectangular guide as shown. Draw the beginning of the porch by adding the vertical and horizontal lines shown. Add straight lines on either side of the porch.

3

Draw two windows on the roof. Add the triangular shapes above the windows. Add long slanted lines to the edge of the roof. Add more slanted and vertical lines to the porch area.

4

Add the window frames and door as shown. Add the vertical railings to the porch. Draw the steps at the front of the porch. Erase any extra lines.

5

Add squares inside the windows. Draw the shutters on either side. Add the squiggly lines beneath the windows. Add details to the top part of the porch. Add the handrails to the steps.

6

Erase most of the guide rectangle you drew in step 1. Add bushes to the entrance, as well as the rectangle on the right. Draw the flag as shown. Erase any extra lines.

7

Draw horizontal lines across the shutters. Add drainpipes on either side of the house and at the right side of the porch. Draw the garden borders as shown.

8

Look at the photograph and the drawing and add as much detail as you like. Finish your drawing with shading. Great job!

World War II

When World War II began in 1939, Kennedy thought England had failed to prepare for the war, and he wrote about that in his final college paper. The paper not

only earned Kennedy one of the highest grades at Harvard, but also it was published as a book called *Why England Slept* in 1940. It became a best-seller.

In 1941, Kennedy joined the U.S. Navy, because he wanted to fight in the war. He was given command of a PT-109, a patrol torpedo boat like the one shown above, in the South Pacific. On August 2, 1943, a Japanese ship sank his boat, killing two crew members. Kennedy and 10 other men survived, clinging to pieces of the sunken boat. When help did not arrive, Kennedy put a wounded crew member on his back and led his men to the nearest island. It took them four hours to swim to the island. Kennedy then swam to another island to get help. Aid finally came about one week later. Kennedy's courage made him a war hero and earned him a medal for bravery.

1

You are now going to draw a torpedo boat. Draw a long rectangle as shown.

2

Draw long curved lines for the sides of the boat as shown. Notice how the lines come to a point at the front of the boat. Draw the shorter lines at the back of the boat.

3

Look carefully at the drawing and at the photograph on the opposite page to help you draw the top of the boat as shown. Notice where part of the boat crosses over the top of the guide rectangle.

4

In this step you will add more details to the top of the boat. Start with the vertical pipes that are near the back. Next draw the curved shapes as shown.

5

Add the remaining shapes to the top part of the boat. Looking carefully at the drawing, add the rest of the details to the back, sides, and front of the boat.

6

Erase any extra lines. Add the squiggly lines to show the spray coming from the water.

7

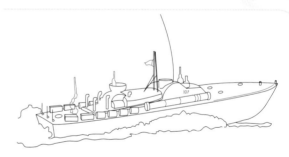

Erase extra lines. Add a flag to the middle of the boat. Draw two shapes toward the back of the boat as shown. Add lines to the front of the boat. Write the number 107.

8

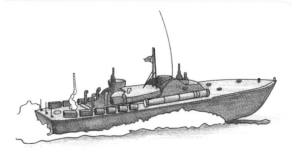

Erase any extra lines. Shade your finished boat. Great job.

Early Political Life

Jack's older brother, Joe Jr., died during World War II. The Kennedy family had thought Joe would follow in both his grandfathers' footsteps and become a politician in the Democratic Party. After Joe died Jack's family pressured him to enter politics. In 1946, Jack ran for Congress as a representative of Massachusetts.

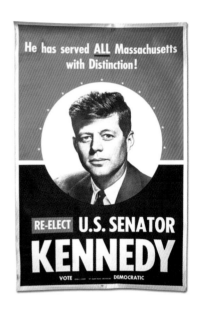

During the campaign he visited factories, homes, and stores to talk to people. His hard work paid off. Kennedy won the election. He was reelected in 1948, and again in 1950. In 1952, he won a seat in the U.S. Senate.

In 1954 and again in 1955, Kennedy had operations for back problems. During his recovery he wrote a book about eight senators in U.S. history who had shown political courage by supporting unpopular causes. The book, *Profiles in Courage*, became a best-seller in 1956, and made Kennedy famous. In 1958, Kennedy ran for reelection as senator and won almost 74 percent of the Massachusetts vote.

1

The poster on page 14 is from Kennedy's Senate reelection campaign in 1958. Begin by drawing a vertical rectangle.

2

Add two smaller rectangles inside the larger one. Then add a circle as shown. More of the circle is in the top rectangle than is in the bottom rectangle.

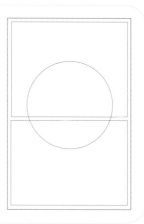

3

Erase extra lines. Draw an oval for the head. Draw a slanted line through the oval. Add circles for the eyes and the nose as shown. Add a line for the mouth. Draw lines for his jacket, his shirt, and his tie.

4

Use wavy lines to draw Kennedy's hair and the outline of his face. Use the guides to draw his eyes, nose, and mouth as shown. Add the lines on his cheeks and his eyebrows.

5

Erase extra lines. Write the words "He has served ALL Massachusetts with Distinction!" above the circle. Make sure that the word "ALL" is in capital letters.

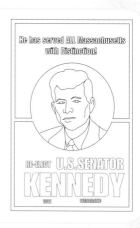

6

Below the circle use capital letters to write the words "RE-ELECT U.S. SENATOR KENNEDY" as shown. Then write "VOTE DEMOCRATIC" in small letters at the bottom of the poster.

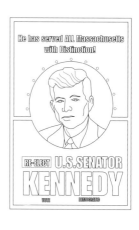

7

Draw 11 tiny circles around the top part of the big circle. Draw a rectangle around the word "RE-ELECT." Add a wavy line to Kennedy's neck and more wavy lines to his hair. Draw tiny circles in his eyes.

8

Now you can shade your drawing of the poster. The darkest parts should be Kennedy's hair, his suit, his tie, and the bottom part of the poster. Great work!

A Charming Wife

The American people thought JFK was one of the most handsome and charming men in Washington, D.C. At a dinner party in 1951, a friend introduced Kennedy to Jacqueline Lee Bouvier. Jacqueline, known as Jackie, was a photographer for the *Washington Times Herald*. Jackie,

like Kennedy, came from a wealthy family and had gone to the best private schools. She was popular in the Washington social scene and spoke French, Spanish, and Italian. Kennedy and Jackie fell in love, and they were married on September 12, 1953. They had two children, Caroline and John Jr.

Kennedy's beautiful wife and young family made him more lovable in the eyes of voters. In 1960, Kennedy was elected president of the United States. As First Lady Jackie met many world leaders. She charmed them with her wit and beauty. She hosted lively dinners, filled with music and art. In February 1962, she gave Americans a televised tour of the White House after she had redecorated it.

1

Start your drawing of Jacqueline Bouvier Kennedy with a vertical rectangle. This rectangle will serve as the guide for your picture.

2

Mrs. Kennedy was called one of the most beautiful women in the world. Draw different-sized ovals for her head, her arms, and her body. Then draw circles for her neck, her shoulders, and her raised hand.

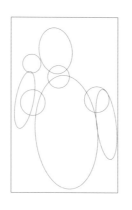

3

Draw three circles as guides for her eyes and nose. Then add a curved line for her smiling mouth. Use five thin ovals to draw her fingers and her thumb.

4

Using the guides from step 3, draw her glove and the rest of her arm. Draw her hair, chin, and hat. Next draw her eyes, mouth, and nose. Add the lines around her mouth and eyebrows. Draw the top part of her jacket.

5

Add a curving line inside the jacket collar. Use straight and wavy lines to finish her jacket as shown. Draw an oval and two circles for the buttons on her jacket. Use the guides to draw her arm. Add more lines for her skirt.

6

Look carefully at the drawing and erase all extra lines. Add the line on the right for the side of her glove.

7

Add lines to the nose and under the eyes. Draw the bit of hair she is brushing back. Add the straight and wavy lines to her glove and jacket.

8

Finish by shading the drawing. The darkest parts are her hair and the edges of her suit. Good work!

President of the United States

At 43 years old, Kennedy was the youngest person and the first Catholic to be elected president of

the United States. Some people feared he was too young to be a good leader. Kennedy pointed to his service as a naval officer and as a member of Congress as proof of his leadership ability and his dedication to the country.

When he became president, Kennedy challenged Americans to do something about the problems facing the nation and the world. "And so, my fellow Americans: ask not what your country can do for you—ask what you can do for your country," he said in his inaugural speech in January 1961.

To help Americans live up to his challenge, Kennedy established the Peace Corps. The program, which still exists, gives people the chance to volunteer in needy countries for two years. Thousands of people have joined the program. When the program was new, some volunteers, shown here, got to meet Kennedy.

1

You are going to draw the Peace Corps logo. Start by drawing a large circle.

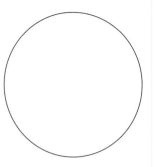

2

Draw a wavy line across the circle as shown. Then draw a slanted line from the wavy line to the bottom of the circle.

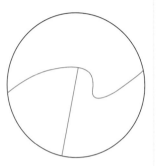

3

Draw a star in the bottom left part of the circle. The star should have five points.

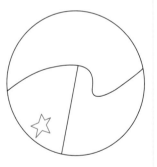

4

Draw a star changing into a bird above and to the left of the star you just drew. Look carefully at this drawing and the photo for help.

5

Draw the shape of a dove above and to the right of the star. A dove is a bird that stands for peace.

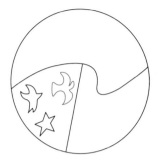

6

Draw four wavy lines in the lower right part of the circle.

7

Use capital letters to write the words "PEACE CORPS" in the top part of the circle as shown.

8

Shade your drawing of the Peace Corps logo. Good work!

The Cold War

By the time JFK became president, the United States was in a race with the Soviet Union to build nuclear weapons. The two nations competed in an effort to prove each had a better system of government than the other. Americans believed in democracy, while Soviets believed in Communism. The conflict was known as the cold war.

JFK also encouraged a more positive kind of competition with the Soviets. In April 1961, Soviet astronaut Yury Gagarin became the first person to circle Earth in space. One month later American astronaut Alan Shepard also traveled into space in a Mercury rocket, shown here, though he did not circle Earth. JFK thought the United States needed to catch up with the Soviet Union. He gave more money and attention to the American space program. His efforts helped the space program move forward. In February 1962, astronaut John Glenn made the first American spaceflight around Earth.

1

Begin your drawing of the Mercury rocket by drawing a tall vertical rectangle.

2

Draw the top part of the rocket inside of the rectangle as shown. Then draw the bottom part of the rocket outside of the rectangle.

3

Draw nine lines across the rocket as shown. Notice how some of these lines are slightly curved.

4

Erase the extra lines around the top part of the rocket. Erase the extra lines at the bottom of the rocket.

5

Draw the lines at the base of the rocket as shown. Some of the lines are straight and someare slightly curved.

6

Draw two small ovals near the top of the rocket. Add wavy lines near those ovals as shown. Then draw five vertical lines on the rocket as shown.

7

Draw four small shapes at the bottom of the Mercury rocket.

8

Erase any extra lines. Finish your drawing with shading. Fill in the space between some of the lines to make stripes on the rocket. Good work.

Trouble in Cuba

Soviet and U.S. relations became more strained in 1962. On October 14, an American U-2 spy plane discovered a secret Soviet plan to build nuclear-missile bases in Cuba and took pictures of the nearly completed bases. Cuba is about 90 miles (145 km) from Florida, so the United States saw Soviet nuclear weapons in Cuba as a risk to American security.

President Kennedy ordered Khrushchev to remove the missiles. He also sent American ships to block Soviet vessels with weapons heading for Cuba. At first Khrushchev refused to admit the Soviets did anything wrong and did not order his ships to turn around. The situation increased the danger of a nuclear war. However, by October 28, Khrushchev ordered Soviet vessels to turn around and agreed to remove weapons from Cuba.

The United States and the Soviet Union were able to avoid a nuclear war in Cuba. However, the two nations remained suspicious of each other.

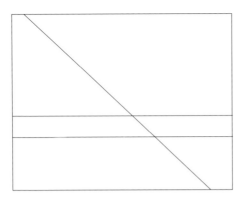

You are going to draw an American U-2 spy plane. Begin by drawing a large rectangle. Then draw a slanted line and two horizontal lines as shown.

2

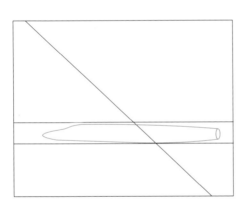

Draw a small oval between the two horizontal lines as shown. Then use curved lines to draw the body of the plane.

3

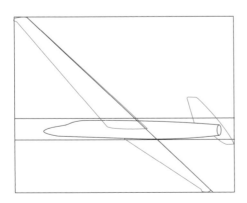

Use curved and slanted lines to draw the plane's wings. Add more curved and slanted lines to draw the tail at the back of the plane.

4

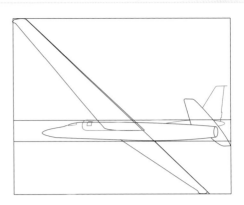

Look carefully at the photo and at this drawing, and add the details to the front of the plane as shown. Then use curved and slanted lines to finish the tail of the plane.

5

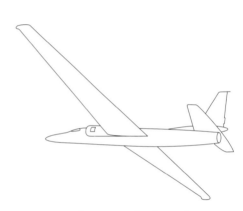

Erase any extra lines, including the rectangle you drew in step 1.

6

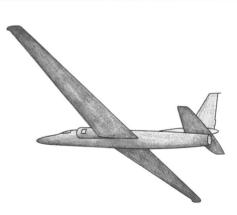

Now shade your drawing of the spy plane. Great work!

Fight for Fairness

As president, Kennedy dealt with conflicts over unfair laws in the South. These laws forced African Americans to sit and eat apart from other Americans. Such laws also often prevented African Americans from voting. By the 1960s, they began to demand equal treatment.

In 1961, a group of people called the freedom riders, shown here, challenged the laws that separated African Americans from other passengers. They boarded buses traveling to the South. When mobs attacked the freedom riders, Kennedy sent U.S. officers to protect them. The next year JFK sent federal troops to the University of Mississippi, where angry crowds blocked an African American man from entering as a student. In 1963, violence broke out in Birmingham, Alabama, as people protested against segregation. The events prompted JFK to make a speech on television calling for equality for all Americans. He also proposed a civil rights bill that would assure that equality. Sadly he did not live to see it become a law.

1

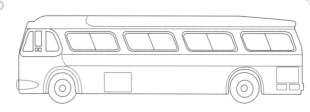

You are going to draw a Greyhound bus like the bus on which the freedom riders rode. Begin by drawing a rectangle as a guide.

2

Use the guide to draw the outline of the bus, including the two arches as shown.

3

Draw two horizontal lines as shown. Add a curving line under the left arch. Add a circle inside the right arch. Draw a medium-sized circle with a small circle inside both arches as shown.

4

Look carefully at the photo and draw the shape of the front window. Add details to the inside of the window as shown. Draw four slanted shapes for the other windows. Add smaller slanted shapes inside each window. Draw a slanted line inside each window as shown.

5

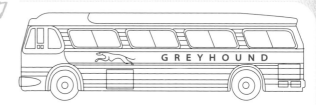

Erase extra lines. Draw the shape at the front of the bus. Add four rectangles to the side of the bus. Add the curved lines over the wheels. Draw a horizontal line toward the top of the bus. Add the curved shape at the top and the horizontal shape across the side of the bus.

6

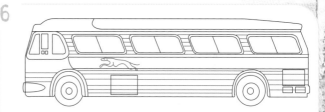

Draw the greyhound dog on the side of the bus with wavy lines. Then draw horizontal lines across the bus as shown.

7

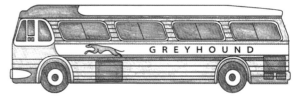

Write the word "GREYHOUND" to the right of the dog you drew in step 6.

8

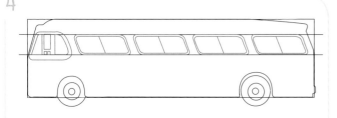

Finish your drawing of the Greyhound bus with shading. The windows and tires are dark. Good job!

A Shocking Day

In 1963, John F. Kennedy began campaigning for a 1964 reelection. On November 22, he and Jackie visited Dallas, Texas.

Cheering crowds greeted the Kennedys as they rode through the streets of Dallas in an open car with Texas governor John Connally and his wife. Suddenly shots were fired, wounding Governor Connally and killing Kennedy. At 46 years old, JFK was the youngest president ever to die in office. Shortly after Kennedy's death, Vice President Lyndon Johnson was sworn into office as the thirty-sixth president of the United States.

A few hours later, Lee Harvey Oswald was arrested for the murder. Two days later Oswald was shot and killed by Dallas nightclub owner Jack Ruby.

JFK's death saddened and shocked the nation and the world. On November 25, 1963, Kennedy was buried in Virginia's Arlington National Cemetery. An eternal flame was placed at his grave site and continues to burn to this day.

1

Start your drawing of Kennedy's grave with a rectangle.

2

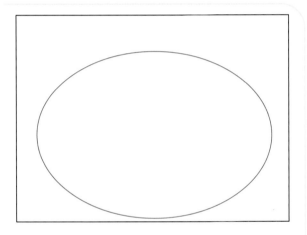

Draw an oval in the lower part of the rectangle as a guide.

3

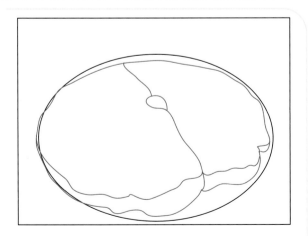

Use the oval guide to draw the wavy outline of the stone. Add wavy lines for the stone's side, its hole, and the crack down its middle.

4

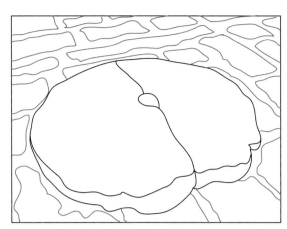

Erase extra lines. Use wavy lines to draw the stones on the ground around the big stone as shown.

5

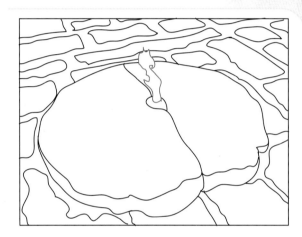

Draw the eternal flame with wavy lines. An eternal flame is a flame that never burns out.

6

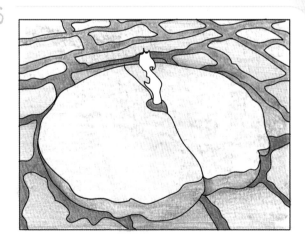

Finish by shading in your drawing. The spaces between the stones are the darkest parts. Great work!

Unfinished Legacy

John F. Kennedy had many plans for the United States that he did not live to see carried out. He wanted to continue improving the relationship between the United States and the Soviet Union. In July 1963, the two nations agreed to a ban on some nuclear-weapons tests.
The treaty appeared to be the beginning of a growing understanding between the two leaders.

JFK was also working on getting congressional support for his civil rights bill before he died. Congress approved the bill in 1964, assuring equal treatment for all Americans.

Kennedy also wanted to boost the American economy, help the poor in the United States and elsewhere, and establish better ties with European and Asian nations. He was hoping for a second term as president in which he could tackle all these issues. Unfortunately he did not get a chance to finish the work he had started.

1

Begin your drawing of President Kennedy with a vertical rectangle. It will be the guide for your drawing.

2

Draw a large oval. Then draw a second oval inside the first oval as shown. Draw two curved lines as guides for Kennedy's shoulder and back.

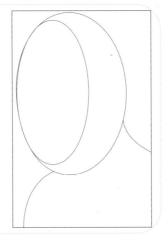

3

Draw the outlines of his hair and his face with wavy lines. Add his ear and chin with more wavy lines. Add slanted guidelines for his mouth and eyes. Add circles as guides for his eyes and nose.

4

Add details to his ear. Use the guides to draw his nose, eyes, and mouth. Draw his eyebrows and the lines below his eyes. Add lines around his mouth as shown.

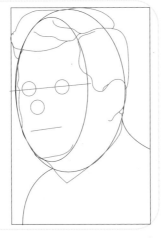

5

Erase any extra lines. Draw a curved line over each of his eyes. Add lines curving up from his eyebrows. Add lines to his neck and his forehead as shown. Add wavy lines to his hair.

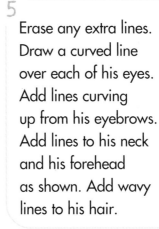

6

Draw his collar and the edge of his jacket. Draw his tie. Add the folds in his jacket with wavy lines.

7

Erase the guide rectangle and the guides for Kennedy's shoulders and back.

8

You are ready to shade your drawing of President John F. Kennedy. The shading is darker in some parts. Great work!

Timeline

1917 John F. Kennedy is born in Brookline, Massachusetts.

1939 World War II begins.

1940 Kennedy graduates from Harvard University.

1941 In September Kennedy joins the U.S. Navy. In December the Japanese attack Pearl Harbor, drawing the United States into World War II.

1943 A Japanese ship sinks Kennedy's boat in the South Pacific, leaving him and 10 of his men in the open ocean.

1946 Kennedy is elected a congressman from Massachusetts. He is later reelected twice.

1952 JFK wins a senate seat. He is later reelected once.

1953 Kennedy marries Jacqueline Lee Bouvier.

1957 Senator Kennedy's book *Profiles in Courage* wins the Pulitzer Prize for biography.

1961 Kennedy becomes president of the United States.

1961 Kennedy creates the Peace Corps.

1962 National Guard troops help protect James Meredith, an African American, at the University of Mississippi.

1963 Kennedy is shot and killed. Vice President Lyndon Johnson takes office as president.

Glossary

asthma (AZ-muh) A condition that makes it hard for a person to breathe.

cemetery (SEH-muh-ter-ee) A place where the dead are buried.

chicken pox (CHIH-ken POKS) A catching illness marked by low fever and breakouts of small, watery, swollen spots on the skin.

civil rights (SIH-vul RYTS) The rights that citizens have.

Communist (KOM-yuh-nist) Belonging to a system in which all the land, houses, and factories belong to the government and are shared by everyone.

competed (kum-PEET-ed) Opposed someone else in a game or test.

declared (dih-KLERD) Announced officially.

dedicated (DEH-dih-kayt-ed) Gave to a purpose.

Democratic Party (deh-muh-KRA-tik PAR-tee) One of the two major political parties in the United States.

inaugural (ih-NAH-gyuh-rul) Of or relating to being sworn in.

introduced (in-truh-DOOSD) Brought into use, knowledge, or notice.

medal (MEH-dul) A small, round piece of metal that is given as a prize.

nuclear (NOO-klee-ur) Having to do with the power created by splitting atoms, the smallest bits of matter.

Peace Corps (PEES KOR) A body of trained people sent to work in other countries for no pay.

photographer (fuh-TAH-gruh-fer) One who takes pictures.

Republican (rih-PUH-blih-ken) Having to do with one of the two major political parties in the United States.

scarlet fever (SKAR-let FEE-ver) An illness that is marked by a fever and breakouts of red spots.

segregation (seh-gruh-GAY-shun) The act of keeping people of one race, sex, or social class apart from others.

survived (sur-VYVD) Stayed alive.

volunteer (vah-lun-TEER) To give one's time without pay.

World War II (WURLD WOR TOO) A war fought by the United States, Great Britain, France, and the Soviet Union against Germany, Japan, and Italy from 1939 to 1945.

Index

Web Sites

Due to the changing nature of Internet links, PowerKids Press has developed an online list of Web sites related to the subject of this book. This site is updated regularly. Please use this link to access the list:
www.powerkidslinks.com/kgdpusa/kennedy/